selected by Ching-In Chen as a winner of the 2019
Essay Press & University of Washington Bothell Book Contest

Poem That Never Ends

Silvina López Medin

ISBN: 9781734498448

Cover artwork by Ingrid Medin
Cover and book design by Blair Johnson

Essay Press is a non-profit 501(c)(3) organization dedicated to
publishing innovative, explorative, and culturally relevant writing.
www.essaypress.org

Distributed by Small Press Distribution
1341 Seventh Street
Berkeley California 94710
spdbooks.org

To my mother

To my sons

CONTENTS

INTRODUCTION

Ching-In Chen

This, Silvina López Medin's *Poem That Never Ends*, a story about linearity of edge.

Fragment between two surfaces. Hint in story.

What if you were raised by refraction? Who lives underneath that surface, gliding closed? Who layers upon layer, variation upon variation? Who protects/against you, inquisitive button of an animal?

One is shaped and molded by quality of half-listening - - ears cupped to preserve and to sieve - - to memory. Rather, this is story about trust and privacy, about glimpsing something not to be shared?   Miniature tuck in word.

Or something to be shared only in one direction.   Into one more hole.

Scrap and overlap, we build texture, a body holding our mothers to form. Pinning her down to scrutiny, perhaps, to give ourselves permission.

For this not really story at all but section cut off across ocean - - just a paragraph settling into a space in its own weird climate.

A recounting of this process - - of drawing out/towards a future less of questions. A spread and stretch of sorts. Sideways approach to getting down hint of curve, blending towards underbelly of understanding.

Where begins a mother and where does giving limit? Full-stop. Anyway, this dance between two desires.

Opposite sides of wall, to ghost through and pause.

Tweak listening glasses again and wait for missing thread to arrive within artifact.

Wait again to peek through artifact's window.

Mark line past rip.

To cut and assemble again, cracked and mingled, and sing into memory's membrane.

POEM THAT NEVER ENDS

But our parents never really have faces.
We never learn to truly look at them.

—Alejandro Zambra, *Ways of Going Home*

–––Dear Ingrid–––baby so we are waiting–––tell her to write to me–––

THE SOUND OF BLINDS BEING PULLED UP
IS THE FIRST SOUND

It's in your hands: the weight of the slats. All slightly bent to one side. As someone that bends with their ear towards the other trying to hear more: what? Your grandmother, like your mother, could only hear 30% of all things. You cross out the word *grandmother*, you'll say your mother's mother. You'd rather have the word repeated—*mother*—build a chain with no missing ring. You're not pulling yet, but it's in your hands, the chain that raises the metal slats. You hear what your mother's mother wouldn't hear: the slats clattering. She, who used to live between blades—her scissors, silent to her—opening and closing on the cloth. Cutting, cutting until what? Until she reached an edge: a pair of eyes looking at her from the other side of the sewing table. Her daughter. Herself. A table—not flat, not smooth, the top filled with pieces of broken wood. Broken: can stick in your skin. A daughter.

A table made of broken things, but varnished, protected. Protective like the blinds you're not yet pulling. **To open and close, to cut** until—to look up and see someone. Not knowing what to do with the weight of a stare or the top of the table: sharp points that don't hurt, but shine, shine, varnished. To separate the cloth just cut **into pieces.** This is **not your daughter,** this is **not you.** And **yet,** you are **a mother**, she's your mother's mother. You're pulling.

BROOKLYN, SEPTEMBER 6, 2018

I asked my mother to send me the **letters** that her mother used **to** send her from Paraguay (where my mother was born) to Argentina (where she moved at 19, where I was born). I estimate she must have received around 126 letters from her mother during her lifetime. Each time she received a letter, she would read it once, and then **rip** it into pieces. She was able to send me only 2 of her mother's letters.

— — —

The 2 letters that she kept were the ones in which, among the usual comments her mother made about her work as a seamstress, **she speaks** about life, **she speaks** about death. One letter is from 1980, the year my brother was born, the year before my mother's father died.

— — —

Her mother abandoned her for 3 years. From the time she was 3 years old until she was 6, my mother lived with her aunts in a town called Piribebuy, 72 kilometers from Asunción, the capital city, 72 kilometers from her mother. During those 3 years she was never visited. My mother never talks about that. *Piribebuy* in Guaraní means **shiver** or *soft breeze*.

BROOKLYN, OCTOBER 18, 2018

I have sent my mother a list of questions about her mother. You can send me the answers on paper or in voice messages, I text her. Wouldn't it be more straightforward just to talk, someone asks. Someone who's not my mother. But we need some deferment, my mother and I. **Look** at this photo from 1980. My father, his father, my mother's father, are looking straight **at the camera**. Yet my mother's mother is looking at me, I am looking at my mother, my pregnant mother is looking at the camera. And **who's behind the** camera? My father's mother, I guess. She must have been trying to fit us all into this tiny rectangle of **glass**: an idea of what the days would look like, when developed.

It rises from the scene, shoots out of **it** like an arrow, and **pierces** me, says Roland Barthes about a central element in photographs. He ends up calling it *punctum*, but I keep the first name he gives it. What is **the wound**, Mother, in this photograph? A question I can think about, not ask. The image my mother captured with her phone. The photograph of the photograph. Like **a memory retold**. Is that the wound? What's lost between the original print version and my mother's digital one. Some resolution. Some precision. The original is on an upper shelf, deep in a box whose lid my mother needs to lift, she needs to get a ladder first, lean it against the wall, stretch her long arms all the way back there, so she cannot reach again now, she says, the original. When I zoom it in on this digital version, it's hard to see any details. So dark the background it gives no indication of place. And then it rises from the scene, shoots out of it like an arrow, and pierces me: the flash. Bouncing off my father's glasses. That light signals what the photographer—my father's mother—was looking at: her son's eyes. **Mother: flash: son**. The glass that's always in between.

BROOKLYN, OCTOBER 20, 2018

I can hear the voice of my friend, the one who used to be my teacher: "The intention is to embody writing, not an anecdote." What is my intention in this "research"? What writing can come out of it? **Stop. Backspace.**

Was that what my mother was doing when ripping each of her mother's letters—breaking the anecdote?

— — —

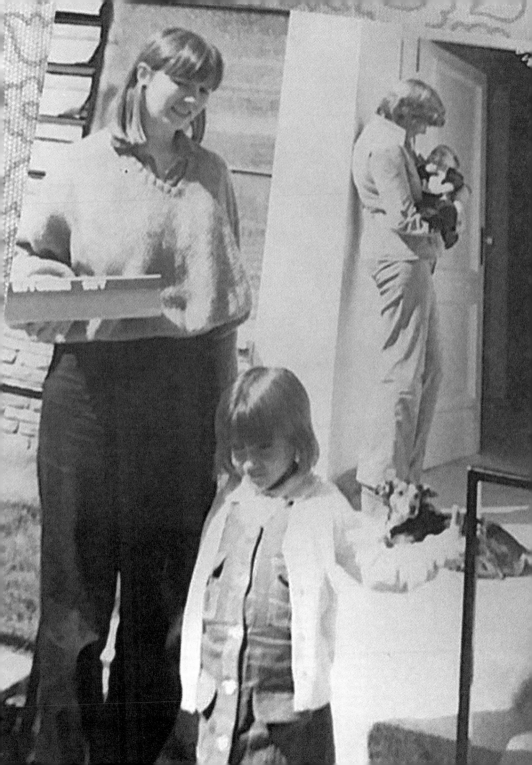

Another scene that I try to write rises. I stop. I can't **inject motion** into it.

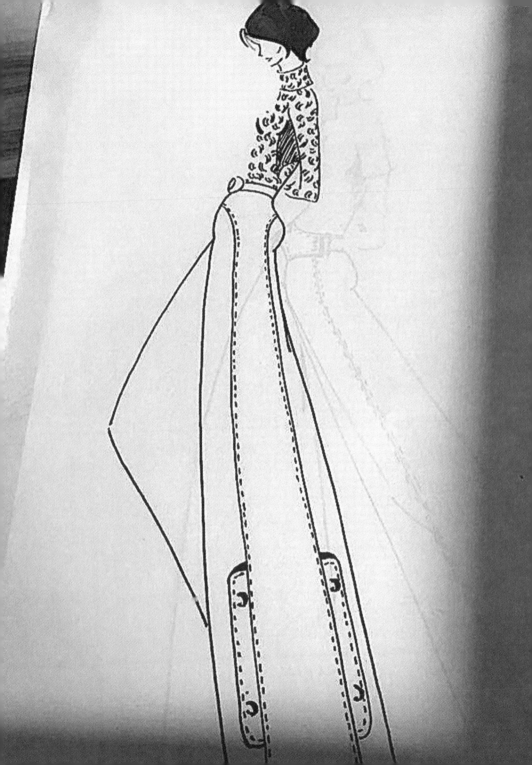

BROOKLYN, OCTOBER 20, LATER

My mother and I, sitting at the kitchen table. I'm 6 and she's teaching me how to shade. Place the pencil onto the edge of things and press. Back and forth, back and forth. And less. And less. Do not darken it all, **do not forget** to let **the light** in.

— — —

I **look again** at the letter from 1980. There my mother's mother says, "Tell Silvina to write to me." I was barely 4, I couldn't write at all. I wonder if the voice I hear when I'm struggling is an echo of that voice: tell Silvina to write.

BROOKLYN, OCTOBER 23, 2018

I gave myself permission to sit each day and write, says a poet who just published her first novel. Night. Bar. A glass in my hand. Two glasses, one in each of her hands, like someone who wears two watches so as not to lose the slightest track. I bend towards her ear, speak. She bends towards my ear, speaks. A rhythm that's outside the rhythm that flows out of invisible loudspeakers. Our glasses are empty and we keep holding them. How did you move to the narrative side of things long enough for a novel to spread, I spill. Here my voice is a whisper, somewhere else would be a shout. It's me speaking and it's my mother, who still can't figure why I can't write poems long enough to blend into something else. She has stopped talking into my ear, the writer, so now I can't hear her. Like my mother, I have to **read her lips** in order to make out how she made it, how writing is a thing **unfolding**. And I can't, I can't make it out.

BROOKLYN, OCTOBER 25, 2018

I am knowing
All about

Unfolding

Mina Loy, "Parturition," excerpt, 1914

When I translated this long poem into Spanish, I had just had my second son. I cannot really say *just*. Too much precision for that period of time. These 3 lines are my favorite lines in the poem, not in my translation.

— — —

WHAT I TELL MY CHILDREN, AND MYSELF, AT BEDTIME

So tall was her father his words
always seemed to come from **afar**.

And then, when she grew,
my mother, moved to a country
that bordered her father's to the south
as if she wanted to keep
looking up to see him.

She would stare at maps,
her old country quietly lying
on top of the new one
like her father used to lay his hand
on her hair.

"I am poem" is the title the teacher shows me. After reading it several times I'm relieved. My son did not write "I am a poem," it's just a fill-in-the-blank exercise, "I am poem."

Then I read the first line "I am---*a son*---."

Those dashes resemble stitches. Or those forms that say, "tear along **the dotted line**."

— — —

to grow
to fold yourself
like **a shell**
to hold
the sound of your surroundings

BROOKLYN, OCTOBER 28, 2018

My mother texts her answers to my questionnaire. Out of 20 **questions**, she skips 4. I can't remember, she answers to another 4. For the rest, the most repeated words are: to sew, to clean. As a postscript she adds: no more speaking of this, what's past is past. If those words were written in a letter, if I ripped it as she ripped almost each of her mother's letters, *what's past* might become a piece of paper **inside a closed fist,** and that would be—torn out of context—one more question, a fist **opening, paper falling**. One more piece to sew, or to clean. I want to call her, I want to tell her I'm not looking at the past, I'm looking at these letters and photographs of the **past, present. I'm not really writing** about your mother or you, Mother, I'm writing about something else. But I don't call her, **I stare at** her virtual plea, I don't know what that **something else** is.

BROOKLYN, OCTOBER 29, 2018

You will not look straight at the camera. Except when you are told to do so.

You will forget.
You will forget.

You will forget that this is you.
I think it can be done.
You will also forget about the camera. But above all, you will **forget** that **this is you**.

You.

Yes, I think it's possible to achieve that from other perspectives, for instance the perspective of motherhood, of your motherhood **lost** in a **dominant nameless** motherhood.

The opening of Marguerite Duras's film *The Atlantic Man*.
I replaced the word *death* with *motherhood*.

BROOKLYN, NOVEMBER 5, 2018

From the darkness of his room one of **my sons** says, "I want mama." I don't turn on the light, I walk until my foot **touches the edge of** his bed: "It's **me**." He repeats, "I want mama."

— — —

to become
almost transparent
the kind of paper you use
only on one side
lest the words tangle
with the back of the words behind

BROOKLYN, NOVEMBER 14, 2018

She boards the plane to Paraguay. She reclines the airplane seat slightly and lets her head fall to the right, so that she can look at a country **receding**, a gray road, fenced houses, a pattern, and then sleep, and look again only 2 hours later at a pattern of red earth, open windows, layers of green, her country. My mother does this at least once a year. She left Paraguay 35 years ago to study design in Argentina. When I was a child, if filled with fury or frustration she could break a cup, a baking dish, a bill, or just repeat *Paraguay, Paraguay*, **a place** to reach towards, not **to grasp**.

BROOKLYN, NOVEMBER 14, 2018, LATER

She was a seamstress, too, I tell my youngest son. My mother's **mother, like my mother.** Do you have two mothers? he asks.

— — —

a shell

a structure that lost the body it **protects**

a sound that is just the extension

of another sound

BROOKLYN, NOVEMBER 15, 2018

She is **a present tense** person, my mother. She does not think about the past. She does not talk about the past, the past as a place you would like to retain, as her mother-in-law would, for instance, someone who refused even to change the water in a flower vase.

— — —

I have to be careful when asking questions, or else she'll say it again: stop.

— — —

She is in Paraguay. She is in the family house where one of her brothers still lives. He is the youngest brother, the one she met when her mother took her back home after 3 years. They used to be 4 siblings, now they are 3. I ask her to ask her brother if their mother kept a journal. I don't think she had time for that, says my mother. Four children, a husband, all her work.

She **stretches the word *all*** as her mother used to stretch the cloth on the table before cutting it. She did not have time for documenting time. On top of that, who keeps a journal? Although she is writing this to me on a screen, I can hear her shouting: "I have never known anyone who keeps a journal."

BROOKLYN, NOVEMBER 17, 2018

Could you describe that? the education specialist asks on the phone. Pause. There's a long dark cable outside, it crosses my studio window from top to bottom, never stops swaying. I can't remember what that cable connects. Could you? Pause. How can I describe him, my son. I start, I stumble, I bump into the "He," say "I."

BROOKLYN, NOVEMBER 19, 2018

A photo of my mother and her brother drinking beer on their patio. This is happening now. The beer on the patio, the photo, my mother sending it to me. In the back, I can see the room where my mother's mother used to work. Instead of the sewing table, a couch, a tall cabinet. Some portraits on a shelf. I can make out **the frames, not the faces**. The only thing that did not change is the wallpaper, as a city seen from afar I cannot tell all its details, I only recognize the general pattern. I know those are bluish grooved vertical lines of flowers. I know it because I remember it.

NEW YORK–BUENOS AIRES FLIGHT DECEMBER 14, 2018

You chose to write precisely what I like less: poetry and theatre, said my mother years ago. I put the airplane seat straight up, open the tray table, my journal on it. Is this poetry. How do you exit such a line? Dead end. If you hit it, hit it again, write it down, someone said. Is this poetry. When you have hearing loss there's a blurred line between statements and questions. When my mother was a child her aunt would take her to the theatre, she would be lost among words she could not grasp, would not look at the stage but stare at the closest exit. Is what you're writing now poetry, she soon might ask. I turn the pages in my journal until I find a quote in a nearby entry.

> Lyric was from its inception a term used to describe **a music** that could **no longer** be **heard**.

A metallic sound precedes the voice on the loudspeaker: we have begun our descent, stow your tray table, pass any remaining service items and unwanted reading materials to the flight attendant.

BUENOS AIRES, DECEMBER 15, 2018

My mother's domain. Her house. Was my house. This is no nostalgic writing. There is no desire to recover what's gone. No need of further separation, of a wall built across. Like the one my mother's brothers once built inside their house in Paraguay **to separate** themselves **from a mother that** was already gone. To separate themselves from themselves. In a house split apart, they stayed.

— — —

We are staying at my mother's house. Sleeping in my mother's sewing studio. I wake looking at a wall covered with shelves, long lines of reels arranged according to color, like my sons' box of pencils. Except these are threads: their ends may pass through the eyes of needles. Needles, pins. Sharp points. Can slip from the hands of a seamstress anytime. **Can stick in your skin** before a red dot expands. Now I am about to get out of bed, now my foot is about to touch the floor.

BUENOS AIRES, DECEMBER 20, 2018

My **mother. I. Split** by the wall that splits the kitchen space. A pass-through: an area where something is missing. Not a hole, an opening. It's intentional. If I speak from this side of the wall, she might hear me. Or not. I'm sitting at the kitchen table with a list of questions. She's on the other side. Crushing plastic water bottles so loud anyone might wonder what's about to burst. Anyone who doesn't know her wouldn't know about her belief that we do not hear what she can't. What scared me as a child: to say anything, to say anything when you can't feel the bouncing of the sound. I'm sitting at the table, waiting for her body to pass across, her mouth to open.

UNDEREXPOSED PHOTO OR WHAT MY MOTHER SAID ABOUT HER MOTHER

both died the same year
it was the same year
her mother and father
don't know
an accident
a field
a sawmill
and her mother a city
and the other the eldest
brought them all
don't know how
there was nothing
don't know well what I know
is hunger
don't know how they lived
don't know anything
they kept
the paper they used to wrap the rice
all the paper
that paper

to write

not even eat

later the eldest started working

mother graduated

but she was not she was like

it was the first time she

and then she met him

do you remember?

she would pass by and father would see her and

they weren't that long

maybe older in truth

don't know

years years

alone in a house

and she met him

what do I know

I'm thinking of a name

— — —

they lived we lived
I was born
in that house in that street
can't remember the name
no no no I think not
don't know what she would do
she started later
to sew at home
don't know
can't remember well
sort of
she started there
he was born first
how can I remember?
he is 11 years older, no
11 months
don't know when but I remember
don't know can't remember
what year she sent me away
not sure
around 2 years old
and don't know the other
born later
between him and I

a miscarriage

and don't know

oh I can't remember

he was born after

I was gone

no no no I cannot remember

not at all

it was going to rain a lot

and then it didn't it looked

like a storm

and in the end

was just gone

this is a double-sided tape it sticks

both ways

mother didn't come

father did

because back in those days

the road was unpaved

they had no car

not like these days

they took him once

the eldest stayed with me

some months

one month

some days
don't know
I never realized they had taken me away

— — —

she must have started at that time
when I went back
I can't remember well
nobody
in the studio all day
father was the one to take us
to the countryside
that's why I like it so much
fields
animals
all
he would take us
often he would get us
would get along
with everybody
and crazy
about the youngest
who?

love
and hate
can't remember that much
I left that house
she didn't want me to sew
never taught me
never let me use the machine
never wanted
anything
by looking at her I looked at her
cutting
night day
can't recall
sewing the only thing
all in order in order she
kept order never to shout
we couldn't tell her
we couldn't make
they quarreled not me
I was always there
later on as I grew
they wouldn't do anything
all the time
they begged her

— — —

like me she gradually lost
her hearing
something
that runs in the family
do you remember?
two hearing two hearing-impaired
no treatment
they had to build we slept
around the corner
they went on building
the house: mother father the youngest
she mispronounces
the teacher said
she didn't say she can't hear
I was the one to grasp
was unable to hear mother
she hears perfectly she said
hearing aid only as a grown up
like me the eldest
never never wanted that
and that was never talked about
at home

the hearing thing
a shared thing? I can't remember
oh the hairdresser's on Saturdays so hot no air
I had to be there hours in her head
rollers I didn't like
I didn't like all that singing side
and her sisters they all sew
and she the most
she was more
father experiments
mother sewing
I'm not sure she used to sew much she just cut
like me and that was
time
the day
the studio
and then design
a course you
are the one to go
go she said
to that country
from here I phoned her I'm
getting married
don't know because I didn't see her

she did not say anything
we did not have a phone
we had to go outside
to a street can't remember its name
mother didn't talk father did
and they came
to the wedding to celebrate
she always the same
she was there and I was here
she would write every two no
every three months the letters
took long
she would write to me
but not tell me she told
of dresses oh
I don't know and
I don't know
I was gone
don't know what they used to do I couldn't hear
I don't remember ever
seeing her crying
people don't talk much there

BUENOS AIRES, DECEMBER 21, 2018

I ask myself one of the questions in the list I sent my mother some months ago. What did your mother look at the most? Her answer: her work. My answer: my mouth. My mother needs my mouth. Needs my lips to read what I say through them. To read me. She doesn't need the sound, just the movement: the opening, the closing, the bending, the shaping of words. Yet she despised my mouth. Scene: my mother and I in front of an elevator mirror, her hand covering my mouth. To see what I would look like without it. Without the piece of me she needed the most. **And** what about **the reverse**.

BUENOS AIRES, JANUARY 7, 2019

On an upper shelf, that's where the photos are, deep in a box whose lid I need to lift, I need to get a ladder first, lean it against the wall, stretch my arms all the way back there, all the way **back towards** them, **the originals**.

I AM WRITING THIS IN MY HEAD, MY HANDS INSIDE GLOVES THAT DON'T MATCH

I lose at least one
from the pair per season
and hold on to the other, that single
glove left behind still contains the lost one.
That is to say
on the winter break I read Pascal Quignard,
in every image there's a missing image,
says he, I add
in every sound there's a missing sound,
say: my mother
how she, because of her hearing impairment,
is permanently reconstructing
sentences from fragments, **isn't that**
writing? I am
walking the nine blocks back home
from the subway, it is -18 degrees
and I'll never know
how to turn that into Fahrenheit or how
at times I focus on something so much as to become
something else. Gloves

prevent us from breaking apart,
gloves are not relevant in Buenos Aires
this cold does not exist
the kind that makes you turn not only your head
but your whole body just to look at
what's coming. I did not write much
back there, just brought
a couple of summer images: my mother and I
at night standing in front a white wall
killing mosquitoes; my mother,
my sons, I, in the backyard,
hurrying to take away the clothes from the clothes line
under light rain.

BROOKLYN, MARCH 1, 2019

My watch does not understand the instability of February. It keeps going, as if today were the 29th, it says: 29. So I have to change it manually. Pull the crown, push it in, pull again until what's hardest to find: the middle position. Then rotate to the correct date: 1. March begins. March is the month in my mother's mother's letter. One of the two my mother kept. The one written in red ink. March, 1980. The date is uncertain, looks like a 9 on top of a 5, or vice versa. As I stare it changes from one to the other and back. So it still moves. Thirty-nine years later, her hesitation exists. A four-day crack. Like the vertical line that marks where the paper was folded. A line that pushes words apart:

 I write | at least   we're doing | well   recovering | quite well

In this letter my mother's mother writes as if she were trying to catch her breath while, like my watch, she keeps going, she uses no period for almost the entire page, for who would dare stop her, she says "your father," she says "his surgery," she says "complication" twice, not as a fact but as something to chase away, she goes on talking about my mother's soon-to-come son, she says "we might be able to travel," then leaves the uncertainty behind: "we'll be expecting your phone call,"

"I'm going to send you," "I'm going to send you," "I'm going to send you." I see her: her body bent over the page that lies on her sewing table, red pen in hand, the same determined posture she had when mopping the floor in the middle of the night, the whole night, back, forth, back, forth. The distorted echo of a far-away dance. Beyond any remnant of dust, any crease or crack in time: her grandson born days later, her husband—until the next year—alive.

PARTIAL VIEWS

After a 1955 family photo

If I turn sideways
        my breath won't reach a surface: won't be exposed, if I move closer
to the pane I might get to see a piece of what they promised: a river
        water flowing in a definite course
or its second blurred meaning: a similar stream
        of something else

If I move the magnifying glass
        away from this photo, **just before the point of blurriness**,
        if I'm patient enough for
both my eyes to focus I can make out the background: a wall
        that marks where that other house ends, the peeling paint
of a distant past: my mother as a newborn,
        her father holding her beneath dark glasses, so much sun
her older brother cries standing against it, and looking down at him though
not picking him up
        her mother, her body split in half
by a shadow of no definite course no definite origin
        so much sun, all of their eyes half-closed

If I turn the photo now
      look at my grandmother's handwriting on the back
the month meticulously spelled, the date unstable.
      She had started to trace a number and then stopped
and traced another number on top of it.
      Had not erased, not crossed out, decided to expose her hesitation

If I go back
      to the point of departure if I face the windowpane and stretch
      myself until I see
what seems to be a stream of something flowing if I let my breath out
      for it to stay on the cold surface long enough
someone like my son
      might draw on it

BUENOS AIRES, MARCH 21, 2019

To wake up back at my mother's studio. I do not make last minute decisions, yet this is one. To come to Buenos Aires for a week. **My sons and I**, not my husband. The alarm clock sounds once more. I must dress up, dip my arms into the suitcase, stir, turn, jolt. My sons' clothes and mine: legs **loosely mingled**. Once more, reaching to confirm what's been forgotten. I have not brought a single shirt, Mother, what can I borrow?

My body in the mirror wearing **my mother**'s black shirt. Loose and tight parts mark the distance between her and **I**. I'm half-dressed as her. I'm half-her. I'm **inside her**.

BUENOS AIRES, MARCH 28, 2019

A leather picture frame on a bookshelf. One of the few things my father kept when emptying his mother's house after she died. It used to be on her night table. A color photo of my brother and I as kids, standing side by side. And hidden beneath it, another photo: my father and his brothers in black and white. Sons-grandsons.

I can't find a phrase that blends. All **under the same framing glass**.

BROOKLYN, APRIL 10, 2019

For my work I have to find the name of the artist of a 1975 book cover. A bookseller sends me a photo of the copyright page I requested. But there's no information on it about the design. The image is a blue square with a white circle inside. It could be a swimming pool seen from above. I get **lost in so much looking**. A year is an edge to hold on to. 1975. The year before I was born. The year before the last coup in Argentina. A beginning of what would last until 1983. The circle becomes a hole, we are inside it, my family and I. Surrounded by the events, though on the surface untouched.

I remember a close-up of a gray-haired man on a black and white TV screen. I remember my father's mother wrapping up her already grown-up child. I remember her asking him what time will you be back, asking everybody when will you be back, do not be late do not forget your coat do not forget your documents. Blinds only half-way up. Slant talk about someone lost. A house nearby one day and one day rubble. Dust. My father's mother preparing me to be picked up by my mom, wrapping me up, layers and layers. I'm standing between sidewalk and street, one foot pressed against the edge, I **cannot breathe**.

MEMORY OF MY MOTHER'S MOTHER AFTER I SCOLD MY SON

A house that holds so many pins. How can such house be safe. What if you step on one. What if you are stepped on. What if you poke, blood. You don't hug but squeeze the waist until it shrinks: **one—more—hole**. To hold the belt in the desired tightness. The yellow measuring tape on your neck like a snake hanging. Or coiled around a body. Writing numbers down on index cards so that nothing will expand nothing will escape you. Warning others not to move too much when encircled by pins on pieces of cloth, temporary fastening.

— — —

— — —

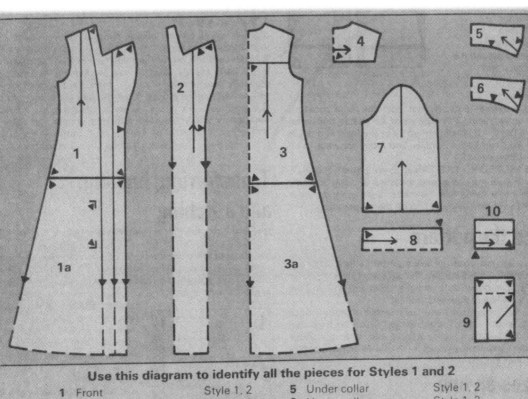

Use this diagram to identify all the pieces for Styles 1 and 2

1	Front	Style 1, 2	
1a	Front extension	Style 1, 2	
2	Front facing	Style 1, 2	
3	Back	Style 1, 2	
3a	Back extension	Style 1, 2	
4	Back yoke	Style 2	

5	Under collar	Style 1, 2
6	Upper collar	Style 1, 2
7	Sleeve	Style 1, 2
8	Cuff	Style 2
9	Pocket	Style 1, 2
10	Pocket band	Style 2

55

In her 1980 letter, before beginning the last paragraph, my mother's mother traces a long line that seems to indicate a deep breath. There is a shift in tone. As if words had been **cut out from someone else's speech**, then assembled. Her use of adjectives and adverbs create sound patterns around thoughts that don't fit her distance from her children. My mother's mother addresses her daughter's approaching delivery date, she says "very well," "all perfectly well," "very humanly natural," "to suffer," "to have the immense joy," "a child," "a filled home, happiness." Years later, before I decided to become a mother, my mother and I would argue about it. Why would anyone not want to have children, she would ask. Our voices raising over each other's. She would question my questioning. She would repeat parts of the letter she didn't rip.

— — —

— — —

LIGHTHOUSE

we were going up and the steps
got narrower, windows
looked to a broader sea
trees like ourselves
clinging to the edges
and the red in some rooftops
broke in the landscape what balance,
all photos
will turn out too dark or too bright: smile
once again, we were going up
hand in hand
steps got higher and higher
feet forced to adjust to stone
unsteady, and that last flight
made of rope
each sole on a knot
up to a door. **We pushed open**
so much wind
I had to take off my earrings
for them not to fly away
I had to pull down your woolen hat

as much as possible, son
as much as possible, I also tell
myself
we walked on the metal structure
a floor of holes
we went in circles
leaning against the cement against each other
wind, water, red tiles on miniature houses,
now we had to go down
and we wouldn't

BROOKLYN, APRIL 17, 2019

La memoria de un sonido is the name of an old literary magazine my friend lends me. *The memory of a sound*. First issue of the two it lasted. Just two, like **a direct sound and its reflection**. Waves crashing against walls. Or a child running into a mother's hard lap.

— — —

When you first realize that your parents are as abandoned as yourself, you are filled with terror, you start asking yourself who's the caregiver here? says Argentine filmmaker Lucrecia Martel in an interview in the magazine.

— — —

Scene: Exterior. Day. Veranda in Buenos Aires. February, 2012. **My mother and I** sitting on a sofa, facing forward. She is talking about her eldest brother, who recently died in a car accident. "Those years my mother left me with my aunts, he was the only one that visited me." She sobs, she's split in half. She's at her aunts' house with her brother. She's here on the veranda with me. I cannot hold the pieces. We're facing forward, I cannot turn around. The sofa fabric is plastic, rigid, I can feel its pattern marking the backs of our thighs.

— — —

It was on February 21, 2012, almost one year since the birth of my eldest son. The phone rang, it was my mother's voice saying, "Enrique is dead. A bus ran over him. He did not hear the horn." No introduction, no details, no real conclusion. A chain of facts, **broken. Pieces scattered**.

— — —

My uncle's hearing impairment was more severe than my mother's. It was **hard** for him **to** articulate most sounds. It was sometimes hard for us to understand, not him, but the words coming from him. Yet he insisted, he did not mind parting words, repeating, asking back. Words would become more material, we could almost **touch** them.

— — —

In the interview, Martel goes on to speak about speech and time: when someone talks, they may use verbs in the present, past or future tense, this temporal quality of words dissolves the idea of consecutive, chronological flow.

In this photo, there is a sepia layer of my mother **and** her brother in the 1950s, sitting close, though not holding each other. And then there is a red spot: the present tense of my mother's nail polish, her fingers holding her phone to take a photo of the photo. Her **fingers holding** themselves.

Who's the caregiver here? I must have thought sitting on the sofa on the veranda by my mother. I must have gotten **lost in the thought**, unable to act.

— — —

I wrote a poem about it. **A piece left out** of some past book. I won't translate it from my native language, so you can at least read this, Mother.

SIESTA

Nos dábamos la espalda
ese sonido ahogado
madre, qué era:
por primera vez te escuchaba llorar,
me quedé quieta
apreté la almohada contra la oreja
la almohada con el olor de tu pelo
no pregunté
no me di vuelta
esperé que pasara pero crecía
tu llanto
entre las dos.
Hicimos lo que pudimos, quedarnos
cada una en su lugar
y en algún momento dormirnos.

BROOKLYN, APRIL 20, 2019

We are moving away from Brooklyn, I tell a colleague. She does not understand where exactly we are moving. The place includes a *t*, a letter whose English version I cannot pronounce. Have I said this is not my language? I repeat it to my colleague, her **not understanding expands**. I point my mouth towards her eyes: I stretch the name of the place between my lips, I mark it, break it, don't let the sound come out.

— — —

This is not my mother's language either. She does not speak it at all. We need some deferment, my mother and I, that I did say before. In this piece **language** is a necessary distance.

— — —

The absence of what's lost or mispronounced. I will probably never be able to get to the *t* that's **at the center of** the place we are moving to. Due to her progressive hearing condition, my mother has lost certain sounds over time, for instance the ending *s* in plural forms. Not the beginning *s* that my name requires.

— — —

I began studying English at 6. In order to show to the class how the *th* is pronounced, the teacher would hold a tissue paper in front of her mouth and repeat: ***mother, mother***. The paper moving **closer and farther away** from her mouth.

BROOKLYN, APRIL 20, 2019, LATER

I'm walking from the office back **home**. It **is** that time of the year when the weather here and the weather in Buenos Aires get close. I'm wearing the airplane headphones I brought from my last trip. They tend to last just a couple of days. This is the day when they start failing. I can only hear music coming from one of the earbuds.

BROOKLYN, APRIL 20, 2019, LATER

During 3 years my mother was left by her mother in a town called Piribebuy, I said at **the** very beginning. What seemed to be a precise fact loses its edges and another layer of memory gradually comes into focus. The town my mother was left in was not Piribebuy. This **other** town— Villarrica—was 100 kilometers farther away from the capital, from her mother. Its main river, Tebicuary, in its Guaraní origin means water that runs through the womb, little running river.

BROOKLYN, APRIL 21, 2019

Clothing is the most intimate inhabitable space that you can actually carry, architecture is an expansion of that, says artist Do Ho Suh. As a child, my mother's mother, like my mother, made many clothes for me, and then one day she gave me a present I had longed for and **I** still **keep**: a tent, **a stitched version of a** house.

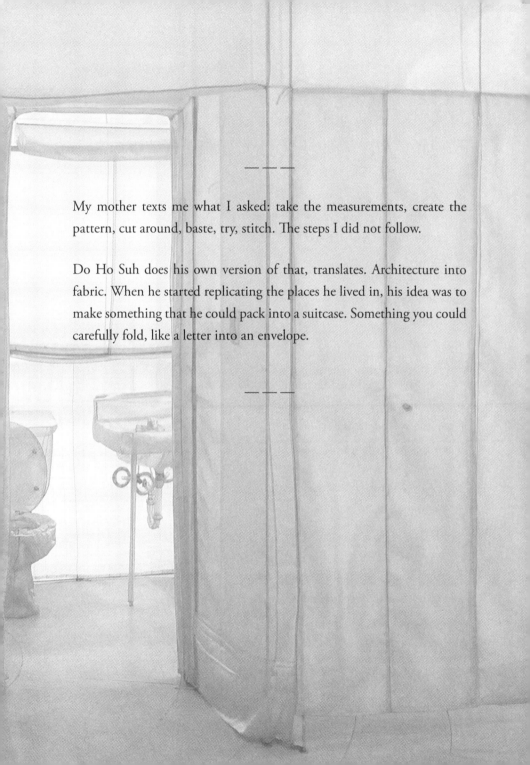

— — —

My mother texts me what I asked: take the measurements, create the pattern, cut around, baste, try, stitch. The steps I did not follow.

Do Ho Suh does his own version of that, translates. Architecture into fabric. When he started replicating the places he lived in, his idea was to make something that he could pack into a suitcase. Something you could carefully fold, like a letter into an envelope.

— — —

THE BLOW OF A HORN DOES AWAY WITH WORDS

my mother on the side, me at the wheel
an excuse for tangential looks

platinum sky-blue
the car ahead contains
my father
and the father
of my sons

something on the ledge behind the backseat slides
from one end to the other
when we change lanes

an object that rubs on a coarse surface
and brings back, as in a tale,
a lost image:
a woman at dawn
wiping a floor that's already shimmering
a gesture that to those tiles adds
nothing

out of nowhere
my mother speaks of that woman, her mother
those years she left me with her sisters
she says, I never asked her
why

like blushing
brought from unexpected closeness
the unknown
redness of a car
comes between us

I blow the horn, tightly
hold the steering wheel
in my hands

My sons and I visit *The Perfect Home II,* a full-scale replica Do Ho Suh built of his former New York apartment. It's made entirely of fabric stitched by hand. We walk within the membranous structure. My sons stay in one room touching the unexpected softness of a light switch. I move on to the following **room**. The fabric is translucent, we are separated by a wall we **can see through**. And we **look** at each other.

CODA

to open and close — to cut — into pieces — not your daughter — not you
— yet — a mother — letters — to — rip — she speaks — she speaks — a —
shiver — look — at the camera — who's behind the — glass — it rises — it
— pierces — the wound — a memory retold — mother: flash: son — I can
hear — stop — backspace — inject motion — do not forget — the light —
look again — read her lips — unfolding — afar — and then — the dotted
line — a shell — to hold — the

questions — inside a closed
— past present I'm not
at — something else —
— dominant nameless
— my son — touches
almost transparent —
grasp — mother like my
— protects — a present
all — could you describe
faces — a music no longer
— from a mother that
skin — mother I split
— back towards — the
don't match — isn't that
does not understand

sound of your surroundings —
fist — opening — paper falling
really writing — I stare
forget this is you — lost
— from the darkness
the edge of — me —
receding — a place — to
mother — a structure that
tense — stretches the word
that — the frames not the
heard — to separate
— can stick in your
— and — the reverse
originals — gloves that
writing? — my watch
the instability — just

before the point of blurriness — my sons and I — loosely mingled — my
mother — I — inside her — under the same framing glass — lost in so much
looking — cannot breathe — one — more — hole — cut out from someone
else's speech — we pushed open — as much as possible son — as much as
possible — a direct sound and its reflection — my mother and I — broken
— pieces scattered — hard to touch — and — fingers holding — lost in the
thought — a piece left out — not understanding expands — language — at
the center of — *mother, mother* — closer and farther away — home is —
the other I keep — a stitched version of a room — can see through — look

POEM THAT NEVER ENDS

Mama is in bed,
eyes wide open, she doesn't turn on the light.

Mama at midnight,
cleans the floor with a cloth over and over.

Mama paints a picture that looks like another one,
she breaks three brushes, not scared of splinters.

Mama is a daughter
a diminutive one, in the backseat of a car
her mother's taking her away
away from her.

Mama at the door
staring at the red scarf on her mother's neck.

Mama writes an entire page to the teacher
words lean forward
as if towards something they're trying to touch.

Mama writes.

Mama is a teacher.

Mama places a pattern on a piece of cloth
cuts around it
cuts a circle on her skin
the scar is a spider.

Mama spins her own cloth
scissors on the side.

Mama turns bangs
into a crooked hem.

Mama teaches me how to draw
trees that bend
pretending movement.

Mama: wound, breath, breeze.

Mama demands stillness,
carries on her neck the weight of a camera.

Mama has lost the voices of birds.

Mama silence

so still
as if she's about to have her photo taken.

Mama got lost under a table.

She moves around the living room
lights turn themselves on over her.

Mama waits in the line that surrounds a dance school
her father's body blocks the door.

Mama draws her family on a paper, she's the tallest one, so tall
her head goes out of the page.

Mama draws all the family
except herself.

Mama paints a self-portrait.

Everything is a self-portrait
she gets tired of.

Mama transports words to another tongue.

Mama changes her own words.

Mama bites her tongue
so many times, so afraid to lose it.

Mama is afraid
to lose it all.

Mama is a tongue.

She splits herself in half because she wants to.

Mama sits on top of someone else
she sways
she expands like a drop of ink on a piece of cloth.

Mama closes her eyes
makes up a prayer to put herself to sleep.

Mama is sinking
no one warns her of false darkness.

Mama wakes up dead.

Mama comes from a land surrounded by more land
comes on the lowest part of a boat
below waterline
she sees fish she doesn't see.

Mama in the ocean with needles on her belly.

Mama is a mother.

Mama is a mother.

Mama keeps the beat of a song she doesn't know.

Mama hugs me and there is always between us
a cushion or a stone.

Mama in summer
sleeps in a nightgown soaked in bathtub water.

Mama wants to return to that summer.

Mama wants to turn around.

Mama on her belly on the sand,
closed tight like an eyelid.

Her face to the sun
to the sun, to the sun.

Mama stays
she asks: how much longer.

Mama has lost another sound.

She insists
how much longer.

Mama paints entire pages.

Mama walks barefoot and steps on the body of a bee.

Mama reads other people's mouths.

Mama lights a fire and places us on top of it
she sings a song that escapes her.

Mama lights a fire
places us around it in winter,
paints our names with ashes.

Mama lights up.

Mama takes us by the hands
lets go of our hands.

Mama asks our names.

Mama sees everything hears everything
remembers everything.

Mama jumps across a puddle that's longer than her legs.

Mama, from where to where.

Mama, our shoelaces keep coming untied
we keep falling.

Mama splits herself in half
she squeezes her mother's red scarf.

Mama wakes up to feed us every night.

Mama doesn't sleep anymore.

Mama sleeps all the time.

Mama is floating.

Mama is sinking.

Mama swims to no shore.

Mama carries us on her back.

Mama cannot see us.

Mama sees everything.

Mama squeezes a scarf,
squeezes our hands
how much longer

IMAGES

Page i: My grandmother's scissors.

Page v: My grandmother, Paraguay, circa 1950.

Page 6: My grandmother's design of her working table.

Page 8: Dress design by my grandmother.

Page 10: 1980 family photo, Argentina.

Page 13: My grandmother's file containing her clients' measurements.

Page 14: 1980 family photo at my grandmother's front door, Paraguay.

Page 16: Design by my mother, circa 1976.

Page 43: My mother and I, Argentina, circa 1979.

Page 44: My mother and a portrait of her, Argentina, circa 2000. Portrait by artist Luis Dottori, 1974.

Page 47: Photo crop of my grandmother and grandfather dancing, Paraguay, circa 1970.

Page 53: Book cover design by Josep Pla-Narbona (Barcelona, 1928).

Page 55: *Dressmaking Pattern,* No. 25 (New York: Phoebus, 1975).

Page 61: My mother and my uncle, Paraguay, circa 1955.

Page 68-69: Do Ho Suh (born Seoul, South Korea, 1962). *The Perfect Home II,* 2003. Translucent nylon. Brooklyn Museum. Photo by Maximiliano Braga.

Page 72-73: Inside *The Perfect Home II.* Photo by Maximiliano Braga.

Page 77: My mother's dress form.

Page 98-99: 1980 letter from my grandmother.

Almost all images are photos of photos, taken by my mother and sent to me on the phone.

REFERENCES

The epigraph of the book is a quote from: Alejandro Zambra, *Ways of Going Home*, trans. Megan McDowell (New York: Farrar, Straus and Giroux, 2014).

Page 11: Roland Barthes, *Camera Lucida*: *Reflections on Photography*, trans. Richard Howard (New York: Hill and Wang, 1981).

Page 19: "Parturition," Mina Loy, *The Lost Lunar Baedeker*, ed. Roger L. Conover (New York: Farrar, Straus and Giroux, 1996).

Page 23: Marguerite Duras, *L'homme atlantique* (Paris: Les Éditions de Minuit, 1982).

Page 31: "Lyric was from its inception a term used to describe a music that could no longer be heard." is a quote from: *The Princeton Encyclopedia of Poetry & Poetics*, 4th Edition, ed. Roland Greene (New Jersey: Princeton University Press, 2012), "Lyric" by Virginia Jackson (826).

Page 45: Pascal Quignard, *La imagen que hoy nos falta*, trans. Julián Mateo Ballorca (Valladolid: cuatro ediciones, 2016). Originally published as *Sur l'image qui manque à nos jours* (Paris: Arléa, 2014).

Page 59: The interview mentioned is "La memoria de un sonido: Una conversación con Lucrecia Martel," by Paula Jiménez España, *Al oído*, September 2011, 4–11.

Page 68: "Do Ho Suh discusses *rubbing/loving*," interview by Julian Rose, *Artforum*, January 17, 2019, https://www.artforum.com/interviews/do-ho-suh-discusses-rubbing-loving-66014.

ACKNOWLEDGMENTS

My sincere thanks to Ching-In Chen for selecting my manuscript and writing an introduction, and to everyone at Essay Press, especially Travis Sharp for his insightful editorial feedback and Blair Johnson for the wonderful design.

Thanks to Wendy Xu who published early versions of "I Am Writing This in My Head, My Hands inside Gloves That Don't Match" and "Brooklyn, April 17, 2019" in *Hyperallergic* and to *Poetry Daily* for featuring "The Sound of Blinds Being Pulled up Is the First Sound."

Special thanks to Ann Lauterbach, Anna Moschovakis, and Asiya Wadud for their kind words of praise.

At NYU, thanks to Deborah Landau, Sharon Olds, Meghan O'Rourke, Terrance Hayes, and Anne Carson. And to my poet friends there, who read early versions of this work and gave constructive feedback. Heartfelt gratitude to Matt Rohrer and to Rachel Zucker, who offered key editorial and extra-editorial layers of support.

Thanks to all my forever friends in Argentina who offered various kinds of support along the way, especially Cecilia Peral for her comments to my questions about language, and Basilio Polijronópulos and Verónica Imbert for their valuable feedback on the book's design. Thanks also to Matvei Yankelevich for his input on specific questions and support. And to Martín Sonzogni for bringing out details in a photo that I didn't even know were there.

Unending thanks to Rebekah Smith, for her vital editorial and aesthetic view in response to each of my questions that seem also to never end.

Thanks to my uncle Carlos Medin in Paraguay for his help finding some images that were very significant to this book.

Deepest thanks to my resistant yet collaborative mother, who also painted the scissors on the cover. She found herself on a journey she didn't expect to take, yet in her own way, joined. Her words and the images she contributed with were crucial to this project.

To my loving family, Maxi, Salvador, and Vicente.

Silvina López Medin was born in Buenos Aires and lives in New York. Her books of poetry include: *La noche de los bueyes* (Madrid, 1999), winner of the Loewe Foundation International Young Poetry Prize, *Esa sal en la lengua para decir manglar* (Buenos Aires, 2014; *That Salt on the Tongue to Say Mangrove*, tr. Jasmine V. Bailey, Carnegie Mellon University Press, 2021), *62 brazadas* (Buenos Aires, 2015), and *Excursión* (Buenos Aires, 2021). *Excursion* was selected by Mary Jo Bang as the winner of the Oversound Chapbook Prize (Oversound, 2020). Her book *Poem That Never Ends* was a winner of the Essay Press/ University of Washington Bothell Contest. Her play *Exactamente bajo el sol* (staged at Teatro del Pueblo, 2008) was granted the Plays Third Prize by the Argentine Institute of Theatre. She co-translated Anne Carson's *Eros the Bittersweet* (2015) into Spanish. Her writing has appeared in *Ploughshares, Hyperallergic, Brooklyn Rail*, and *MoMA/post*, among others. She holds an MFA in Creative Writing from NYU and is an editor at Ugly Duckling Presse.

Guasacii Marzo

que mañana va a ser

te escribí por lo menos

líneas para hacerte sabe

pasando bien, tu papá

sando pasándote bien

espero que no se ponga

que no le venga ninguna

en el futuro ya que e

así cualquier complicación

el muy delicado, pero es

muy bien, y pienso que

podríamos ir después

bebé para conocerlo

así que esperamos tu

nos compres Idalia ya

de voy a mandar m

otra cuega te va ma

zada que es una

1980

...guél

...norechando

...aldirar

...poeas

...estamos

...tá necupe-

...peración

...ndo para

...plicació

...lativo,

...úa ser para

...ral el está

...así sigue

...llegué el

...mocerla,

...marla, ...gu

...el bebé, qu

...muy lim...

...la una f...

...illa para...